BLUE BANNER
BIOGRAPHY

# ADELE

Mitchell Lane        *Tammy Gagne*

PUBLISHERS
P.O. Box 196
Hockessin, Delaware 19707
Visit us on the web: www.mitchelllane.com
Comments? Email us: mitchelllane@mitchelllane.com

**Mitchell Lane**
PUBLISHERS

Printing     2          3          4          5          6          7          8          9

**Blue Banner Biographies**

| | | |
|---|---|---|
| Adele | Ice Cube | Miguel Tejada |
| Alicia Keys | Ja Rule | Nancy Pelosi |
| Allen Iverson | Jamie Foxx | Natasha Bedingfield |
| Ashanti | Jay-Z | One Direction |
| Ashlee Simpson | Jennifer Hudson | Orianthi |
| Ashton Kutcher | Jennifer Lopez | Orlando Bloom |
| Avril Lavigne | Jessica Simpson | P. Diddy |
| Blake Lively | J. K. Rowling | Peyton Manning |
| Bow Wow | Joe Flacco | Pink |
| Brett Favre | John Legend | Prince William |
| Britney Spears | Justin Berfield | Queen Latifah |
| Bruno Mars | Justin Timberlake | Rihanna |
| CC Sabathia | Kanye West | Robert Downey Jr. |
| Carrie Underwood | Kate Hudson | Robert Pattinson |
| Chris Brown | Katy Perry | Ron Howard |
| Chris Daughtry | Keith Urban | Sean Kingston |
| Christina Aguilera | Kelly Clarkson | Selena |
| Ciara | Kenny Chesney | Shakira |
| Clay Aiken | Ke$ha | Shia LaBeouf |
| Cole Hamels | Kristen Stewart | Shontelle Layne |
| Condoleezza Rice | Lady Gaga | Soulja Boy Tell 'Em |
| Corbin Bleu | Lance Armstrong | Stephenie Meyer |
| Daniel Radcliffe | Leona Lewis | Taylor Swift |
| David Ortiz | Lil Wayne | T.I. |
| David Wright | Lindsay Lohan | Timbaland |
| Derek Jeter | Ludacris | Tim McGraw |
| Drew Brees | Mariah Carey | Tim Tebow |
| Eminem | Mario | Toby Keith |
| Eve | Mary J. Blige | Usher |
| Fergie | Mary-Kate and Ashley Olsen | Vanessa Anne Hudgens |
| Flo Rida | Megan Fox | Will.i.am |
| Gwen Stefani | | Zac Efron |

**Library of Congress Cataloging-in-Publication Data**
Gagne, Tammy.
  Adele / by Tammy Gagne.
     p. cm. — (Blue banner biographies)
  Includes bibliographical references and index.
  ISBN 978-1-61228-314-2 (library bound)
  1. Adele, 1988– —Juvenile literature. 2. Singers—England—Biography—Juvenile literature. I. Title.
  ML3930.A165G35 2013
  782.42164092—dc23
  [B]
                                                                                        2012018301
eBook ISBN: 9781612283852

**ABOUT THE AUTHOR:** Tammy Gagne is the author of numerous books for both adults and children, including *What It's Like to Be America Ferrera, Day by Day with Beyoncé, We Visit Mexico, Ways to Help Chronically Ill Children,* and *How to Convince Your Parents You Can Care for A Pet Racing Pigeon* for Mitchell Lane Publishers. As an avid volunteer, one of her favorite pastimes is visiting schools to speak to kids about the writing process. She lives in northern New England with her husband, son, dogs, and parrots.

**PUBLISHER'S NOTE:** The following story has been thoroughly researched, and to the best of our knowledge represents a true story. While every possible effort has been made to ensure accuracy, the publisher will not assume liability for damages caused by inaccuracies in the data and makes no warranty on the accuracy of the information contained herein. This story has not been authorized or endorsed by Adele.

PLB

*Blue Banner Biography*

Adele won six Grammy Awards in 2012. She went home with every Grammy Award for which she was nominated. The question on everyone's mind that evening was whether her voice would be the same after having vocal cord surgery months earlier.

# CHAPTER 1

# She Gets It From Her Mum

She stood on the stage at the 2012 Grammy Awards looking as beautiful as ever. Her hair, her makeup, her tasteful black dress . . . everything about Adele is timeless. If we didn't know better, we could easily believe that the year was 1962, or even 2062. When Adele sings her songs, they sound like they have always existed. At the same time, they seem fresh and like nothing we have ever heard before.

The question on everyone's mind this evening was: Did she still have that powerful voice that made her famous? It had been months since she had performed in public. Vocal cord surgery had forced her to take a break from singing. It had left her fans wondering if she would return to singing at all. Even if she did return, there was no guarantee that she would sound the same.

She began singing her smash hit, *Rolling in the Deep*, a cappella. So far, so good. Then, she stopped. Had it been too much for her? Did she try to return too soon? Before her fans could gasp in concern, the music began booming behind her, and Adele continued with her song. It was just a tease; her voice sounded as strong and as soulful as ever.

*Adele doesn't just sing her songs. She feels them, and so do her listeners. Many of her songs are about heartbreak and pain. People respond to her honest lyrics, because they can relate to them.*

Like many other well-known performers, Adele now goes by just a single name, but this wasn't always the case. She was born Adele Laurie Blue Adkins in London, England, on May 5, 1988. Her mother, Penny, was just 19 years old when she gave birth to Adele. Penny's parents would not help their daughter when she became pregnant unexpectedly. They thought it was important for Penny to take care of herself and her young daughter.

Adele's father, Mark Evans, was from Wales. He left Penny and returned to Wales when Adele was just three years old. "It's fine," Adele told *The Observer* in 2008. "I don't feel like I'm missing anything." In an interview with the

*Daily Mail* that same year, she added, "Some people make a big deal about coming from a single-parent family, but I know loads of people who grew up without having their dads around." Clearly, that same independence that Penny learned as a young adult has been passed on to her daughter.

In recent years, Mark has given multiple interviews with the press about his now-famous daughter. He speaks fondly of the short time he was a part of Adele's life. He recounts proposing to Penny when he found out she was going to have a baby. She turned him down, insisting that they were too young for marriage. He also describes cradling an infant Adele in his arms while they listened to artists like Ella Fitzgerald and Louis Armstrong together. He even thinks that he influenced her musical style by playing his favorite music around her. Adele doesn't believe her father has had much influence on her. On the contrary, she told *Rolling Stone* rather bluntly that he has no right to speak about her at all.

> When Adele sings her songs, they sound like they have always existed . . . they seem fresh and like nothing we have ever heard before.

Adele has great memories of growing up with her mother. Before Adele was born, Penny had been an art student. Raising a child on her own, though, changed her plans of becoming an artist. Instead, she worked various jobs to support her family of two. "She never, ever reminds me of that," Adele told the *Daily Mail,* but she added, "I try to remember it."

Mother and daughter moved around a lot, something Adele told *Rolling Stone* she loved. "I think that's why I can't stay in one place now. I don't think of my childhood like 'Oh, I went to ten different schools.' My mum always made it fun."

She credits her mother for leading her to some of her favorite musicians. Penny introduced her to artists like Mary J. Blige, Lauryn Hill, and Alicia Keys. Adele discovered the music of Etta James in the bargain bin of a record store. This

*Adele attended the Keep A Child Alive 5th Annual Black Ball in New York City with Alicia Keys. Alicia was one of Adele's earliest musical influences. Her mum used to play Alicia's music at home.*

find was a bargain indeed. She described the discovery to *Rolling Stone* as "the first time a voice made me stop what I was doing and sit down and listen." She says it took over her entire mind and body. Little did Adele know at the time that her voice would one day do the same thing to countless others.

# CHAPTER 2

## Student of Soul

**M**usic was a big part of Adele's young life. Penny took her daughter to her first concert when she was just three years old. They went to see The Cure play at Finsbury Park. On Friday nights Adele's mother would let her stay up late to watch *Later,* a music program on the British Broadcasting Channel (BBC). When Penny had friends over for dinner, the evenings would often end with a five-year-old Adele standing on the dining room table singing a new song she had learned.

Adele remembers fondly how proud her mother was of her. Penny told her daughter she was amazing. Adele was likewise quite proud of her mother. Adele recalls that when she performed, Penny would arrange regular household lamps to shine on her little girl like a spotlight.

Adele began writing songs as soon as she could read and write. When other kids were learning their ABCs, Adele was penning poetry. Her father recalls Adele visiting him in Wales when she was about four. At the time she had a small acoustic guitar that she was teaching herself to play.

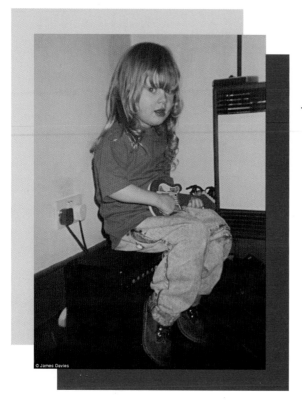

*Adele has been performing since she was a small child. Her mother would invite friends over and ask Adele to sing new songs she had learned. Adele began teaching herself to play guitar at the age of four on a toy instrument.*

© James Davies

Although Adele says she never really knew her father, she was very close with her grandparents on her father's side. She spent a lot of time with her grandfather, John Evans, in particular. In 2011 Adele told *The Scotland*, "He just loved my mum, and because my dad wasn't in her life, they completely took her over as their daughter."

When Adele was seven years old, her father and his new girlfriend had a son named Cameron. Adele and her half-brother took to each other right away, and they have a good relationship today. In the interview with *The Scotland*, she said they look like they could be twins. "We're identical, same hair and everything." The only difference between them, she adds, is that he is very shy.

Penny came from a large family. Adele has numerous aunts, uncles, and cousins. She is one of fourteen grandchildren on her mother's side.

Adele grew up in the borough of Haringey. Her neighborhood, called Tottenham, is reported to be the most ethnically diverse area in England. More than 100 different ethnic groups live there, speaking nearly 200 different languages. Arguments between the different groups have caused riots in the area many times over the last several decades.

When Adele started primary school in Tottenham, she was one of the only white children there. This didn't bother her too much. "I stopped noticing after a while," she told *The Observer*. Being around so many people from different cultures had a big effect on her musical tastes. She especially loved soul music.

As Adele got older, her musical talent grew with her. In addition to the guitar, she now played the clarinet and sang. When she was 14, she was accepted into a performing arts high school in London. The BRIT School had a student body that read like a who's who of the future music industry. Leona Lewis, Jessie J, Kate Nash, and Amy Winehouse all went there. "It was a bit like [the movie] *Fame*," Adele told *The Telegraph*.

*Adele began writing songs as soon as she could read and write. When other kids were learning their ABCs, Adele was penning poetry.*

Classmates remember her as a talented but not particularly driven girl. Ben Thomas, who now plays guitar for Adele, went to school with her at BRIT. He recalls that some of the students there pushed really hard to get into the music business. It was obvious how much they wanted it. "Adele never really had that," he told *Rolling Stone* in 2011.

"But she was a good performer, and everyone would be completely silent and in awe when she performed."

Adele loved music, but she didn't expect to make a career out of it. When she was younger, she had dreamed of becoming either a fashion reporter or a heart surgeon as an adult. It was one of her classmates at BRIT who changed Adele's future during her last year at the school. This friend uploaded some of Adele's music to the social web site Myspace. Adele had recorded the three-track demo as part of a class assignment.

Managers from several record labels found her music and liked what they heard. Adele began receiving emails from the managers asking to meet with her, but "I didn't know who to believe," Adele told *Pollstar*. "I didn't know if they were genuine." Eventually, her mother convinced her to call one of the labels.

Adele agreed to meet with an executive from XL Recordings. She asked Ben to join her, though, just to be safe. She knew that people on the internet sometimes weren't who they said they were.

Even after the label turned out to be real, Adele still didn't quite realize what was happening. At first she thought the label might offer her an internship, which is a non-paying job that young people often take in order to learn more about an industry. She had no idea that in a just a few short months she would be signing her first record deal.

# CHAPTER 3

## *19 and Counting*

*A*dele titled her first album *19* for the age that she was when she began recording the CD. It was released in early 2008. Its first single, "Hometown Glory," was an instant hit in her home country. Americans also seemed to like Adele, but it would take some time before she would become as popular in America as she is today.

Her album appeared on the album chart at Number 56 in the United States, and from there it began dropping. It didn't seem like Adele was going to be the huge success in the U.S. that she was in England. Then she was offered a chance to perform as the musical guest on *Saturday Night Live (SNL)*. Adele's performance on the television show would take place the same evening that vice-presidential candidate Sarah Palin was scheduled to appear. Adele knew that this meant millions of Americans would be watching.

"I was sitting in my dressing room having my makeup done," she recalled in *Rolling Stone,* "and I thought, 'If you nail this, this could be one of those moments in a career.'" Although then-Governor Palin may have been the one who initially attracted the audience, Adele was definitely part of

Adele won the Critics Choice Award at the 2008 BRIT Awards in London. Her music became an instant hit with the people of England. It took her a little longer to win over American fans, but she has definitely done it.

the reason they kept watching—and listening. She performed two songs, "Chasing Pavements" and "Cold Shoulder," for the episode. More than 14 million people tuned in to the show—and obviously liked what they heard.

Adele's manager, Jonathan Dickins, described the whirlwind series of events that took place following the appearance in the *Rolling Stone* article. "When we did the performance on *SNL*, we were at Number 40 on iTunes. The following morning we were at Number Eight. When I got off the plane in London, we were at Number One."

In 2009, Adele won Grammy Awards for Best New Artist and Best Female Pop Vocal Performance for "Hometown Glory." At home, the BBC named her the Sound of 2008 for *19.* Her success story was just beginning.

*Americans also seemed to like Adele, but it would take some time before she would become as popular in America as she is today.*

Adele was 21 years old when she recorded her second album, and in keeping with her theme from the first album, she titled it *21.* Released in early 2011, it sold more than 352,000 copies in its first week. Clearly, Adele was here to stay.

The single "Rolling in the Deep" was especially popular. As Atlanta's Wild 105.7 program director J.B. Wilde explained to *Rolling Stone,* "It really resonated, especially with women. She's not just singing the song, she's feeling it. A year ago, if you said Adele would get played on our station, the answer would have been 'no way.' But Adele wouldn't be denied."

Rick Rubin, the co-head of Columbia, Adele's North American label, isn't surprised at all by her success. He told

Adele's 2008 peformance on **Saturday Night Live** sent her to the top of the iTunes chart. The day she appeared on the show, she was ranked at Number 40 on iTunes. By the next morning, she had risen to Number 8.

*Rolling Stone,* "People assume something gets successful by fitting in, but the greatest and most revolutionary artists don't fit. Good music transcends what fits in the culture."

In an era where a lot of the music we hear on the radio sounds the same, Adele definitely stands out. Christian Tattersfield, the CEO of Warner Brothers in England, believes that Adele's success shows that people want to hear more unique artists on the airwaves. In a 2011 *Music Week* article, he called her success "a wakeup call for all record companies to sign and develop better artists."

As Adele's second album was climbing the charts, *19* was still holding strong. Likewise, "Rolling in the Deep" remained high on the charts when the second song from *21* was released. When that song, "Someone Like You," made the top five, Adele tied an impressive record in the music industry. She became the first artist since John Lennon to have two top five singles and albums on the charts at the same time. It had been thirty years since John Lennon's songs "Woman" and "Imagine" shared the singles chart, while his albums *Double Fantasy* and *Imagine* appeared together on the album chart.

The 2012 Grammys ceremony belonged to Adele. She won every award for which she was nominated—six in all. These honors included Album of the Year (*21*), Pop Solo Performance ("Someone Like You"), Pop Vocal Album (*21*), Record of the Year ("Rolling in the Deep"), and Song of the Year ("Rolling in the Deep").

> *"A year ago, if you said Adele would get played on our station, the answer would have been 'no way.' But Adele wouldn't be denied."*

# CHAPTER 4

## Behind the Voice

**W**ith her reputation for saying exactly what she thinks, Adele's personality is just as refreshing as her music. Dickins believes that her honesty is part of what comes through in her music. As he told *Billboard* magazine, "The key to great singers is believing every word they sing. And I think you believe every word that comes out of Adele's mouth."

Perhaps people can relate to Adele's words, because she seems like one of them. She told the *New York Post* that people often say that she reminds them of their mothers or sisters. "I always feel like I'm the only person who is feeling what I'm feeling, and there's . . . millions and millions of other people who feel exactly the same. So if my record can make someone else say, 'Oh, thank God, yes, she knows exactly what I'm talking about,' then my job is done."

Adele wrote many of the songs on *19* about her breakup with her first serious boyfriend. Richard Russell, the owner of XL, believes that people relate to Adele's songs about being hurt. He calls her subject matter very honest.

The songs from her second album were inspired by the end of her second romantic relationship. She admits that many of her songs are sad. She even joked to *Rolling Stone* that if she were ever in a happy relationship there might not be any more music. "My fans will be like, 'Babe, please, get divorced!'"

The truth is, singing songs about a real-life broken heart can be difficult. At times Adele has been close to tears at the end of a performance, sometimes even needing to turn away from the cameras. Still, she seems grateful for her experiences. Speaking of the lost love who was the inspiration behind *21*, she told *Rolling Stone*, "He put me on the road I'm traveling on."

The emotional nature of Adele's songs isn't the only thing that Adele finds challenging about performing them.

*Singing isn't Adele's only passion; she also loves to play the guitar. She prefers smaller venues to large arenas. She has said she will never play large music festivals due to her intense stage fright.*

She also suffers from severe stage fright. One might think that this problem would ease with time, but Adele says that it only gets worse the more she performs. "One show in Amsterdam, I was so nervous I escaped out the fire exit," she admitted to *Rolling Stone.* "I've thrown up a couple of times . . . I don't like touring. I have anxiety attacks a lot."

The worst part of Adele's stage fright is that it doesn't go away until the show is completely finished. "My nerves don't really settle until I'm offstage." She knows that people are spending their money to come to her concerts and she worries about disappointing them. "It's such a big deal that people give me their time," she explained to *Rolling Stone.*

Adele is also extremely afraid of flying. She confides that she is convinced that she is going to die every time she boards an airplane. Traveling for performances is part of her job now, which means she has to face her fear of flying head-on.

One thing Adele doesn't worry about is how she looks. "I've never wanted to look like the models on

magazine covers," she announced proudly to *People* magazine. "I wasn't brought up like that. I hate when something is all visual and not about the music. I'm not one of those artists, so I don't have the pressure."

Looks also aren't what attracts Adele to other people. "I'd rather date an ugly, hilarious guy than Leonardo DiCaprio," she insisted to *People.* "Humor keeps relationships together." She adds that American men usually don't get her dry, sarcastic sense of humor.

When it comes to fashion, Adele says she opts for comfort over glamour. She loves bulky turtleneck sweaters and black, well, black anything. Even when she is dressed for upscale events, she is usually wearing black. She does like glamorous makeup, however. She told *In Style* magazine, "When I'm working, I go for very dramatic makeup. I love contouring . . . with lots of blush on my cheeks."

Adele knows what she likes and what she doesn't. This is true with her music as well as with every other part of her life. She is extremely grateful for her musical success, but sometimes she dislikes all the attention. She cannot even leave her house in England without causing a media frenzy. When she tried to visit London's Victoria and Albert Museum, she received so much attention that she had to leave. "That's not why I got into music," she pointed out to *Entertainment Weekly* in 2011.

One thing stardom does allow Adele to do is spread the word about causes that are important to her. One of these is

> *The truth is, singing songs about a real-life broken heart can be difficult. At times Adele has been close to tears at the end of a performance.*

# ADELE 21

**TO ALL PROMOTERS OF THE CURRENT ADELE NORTH AMERICAN TOUR:**

**Please see below an important update to our guest ticket policy:**

All guests at all Adele shows will be asked for a minimum donation to charity of $20.00 per person, in cash, when they collect their tickets. There will be no exception to this rule.

**We will also expect that all guests of the Promoter and/or Venue to also make the same donation when collecting their tickets.**

There may be occasions where the donation may have been made on behalf of the guests prior to them collecting their tickets. If this is the case, "Donation Paid" will be clearly marked next to their name on the Artist guest list.

At Adele's personal request, all money collected will be donated to
"SANDS" www.uk-sands.org
This is a charity that is dedicated to "supporting anyone affected by the death of a baby and promoting research to reduce the loss of babies' lives"

We will require your help and assistance to implement this policy at the box office.
Please provide the services of an experience, capable person who can deal with the administration and cash handling aspects of our guest list requirements.
All cash to be given to Adele Tour Manager at the end of the show.
All relevant guest lists, clearly marked to indicate who has paid and who has not collected their tickets, to be returned to Adele Tour Manager at the end of the show.

We will provide documentation from the "SANDS" charity confirming that we are authorised to collect money on their behalf.

On our recent UK and European Tour we raised over $13,000.00 from donations made by guests and we hope to continue this good work in North America.

Thank you for your help with this – we believe that this is a very worthwhile cause.
Best regards


Zop – Tour Manager, Adele

ADELE Rider
Updated July 18, 2011

Sands, a British charity that provides counseling and support to anyone affected by the death of an infant. The group also raises money for research to prevent this type of loss. Adele insists that anyone who receives a free ticket to one of her concerts make a donation to Sands — and when Adele insists, people listen.

# CHAPTER 5

## Facing Challenges

*W*hen Adele thinks about her musical success, she credits the high school where she made that life-changing demo. "I think I do owe it *completely* to the BRIT School for making me who I am today, as cheesy and embarrassing as it may sound," she told *Blues & Soul Online*. "Because, while my mum is the most supportive mum on *Earth,* she wouldn't have known how to *channel* me. With her I'd probably have gone down the classical music route or maybe Disney or musical theater . . . But at the BRIT School I found my direction, because the music course was really wicked."

Many years have passed since that first concert in Finsbury Park. Adele hasn't forgotten it, though. She pays a small tribute to The Cure — and likely to her mum as well — with her cover of the band's "Lovesong." Adele's version appears on her album *21.*

Adele has been very inspired by country music artists since visiting the United States. While on tour, she listened to musicians like Garth Brooks, Dolly Parton, and June Carter. It was her bus driver, who is from Nashville, who introduced her to country and bluegrass music. "It's not part of our culture in England," she admitted to the *New York Post*. "I'm completely clueless to it."

One of her favorite country groups is Mumford and Sons. "They're closer to how I feel about Etta James than anyone," she explained to the *New York Post*. "Whenever I hear their songs, whenever I hear Marcus Mumford's voice . . . it goes right through me . . . like, literally goes into my chest and beats me up—and makes me completely fearless."

> *Many years have passed since that first concert in Finsbury Park. Adele hasn't forgotten it, though.*

Her bold personality comes through once again when she talks about marketing gimmicks. Sometimes companies offer artists money to mention their products in their music, but Adele vows that she will never allow her music to be used for this type of tie-in advertising. She sees this kind of deal as selling out. She also said that she was extremely upset when her first album was re-released with extra tracks on it. She doesn't believe that a re-release should be used to make money at her fans' expense. She won't allow it to be done again.

Although Adele shares some of her most personal struggles through her music, you won't find her Tweeting about them. She stopped posting on Twitter around the same time she rose to fame. Adele doesn't seem to hold anything back when she grants an interview, but she doesn't think she needs to be in everyone's face all the time. "I don't ever want my personality to be bigger than my music," she told *Rolling Stone*.

You also won't be seeing Adele at any of the large-scale musical festivals. She doesn't even enjoy playing large arenas that house tens of thousands of concert-goers. Her stage fright makes smaller venues much more inviting to her.

She has come up with a strategy for dealing with her fear of performing, though. Adele has created an alter ego named Sasha Carter, an idea she borrowed from another famous singer. "I was about to meet Beyoncé," Adele recalled to *Rolling Stone*, "and I had a full-blown anxiety attack. Then she popped in looking gorgeous and said, 'You're amazing! When I listen to you, I feel like I'm listening to God.' Can you believe she said that?" When Adele was faced with performance jitters later that night, she asked herself what Beyoncé's famous alter ego, Sasha Fierce, would do. "That's when Sasha Carter was born." Part Sasha Fierce and part country role model June Carter, Adele's other personality

*Beyoncé helped Adele deal with her enormous stage fright. When Adele performs, she imagines that she is a character named Sasha Carter — much like Beyoncé's alter ego, Sasha Fierce.*

# ADELE

### LIVE AT
## THE ROYAL ALBERT HALL

now joins her at performances to help her battle her stage fright.

The scariest thing Adele has faced since becoming an international star was a vocal cord hemorrhage. She underwent surgery for the injury in late 2011. After canceling her second run of US tour dates in October of 2011, she explained her decision to her fans on her web site. "Singing is literally my life. It's my hobby, my love, my freedom, and now my job. I have absolutely no choice but to recuperate properly and fully, or I risk damaging my voice forever."

*Adele's fans missed her dearly when she had to take time off for vocal cord surgery. They were thrilled when she returned to the stage in 2012.*

Her fans were sad to see her step away from the stage as she nursed her injury, but most of them understood. When she finally returned to the stage at the Grammys in February of 2012, nearly 40 million people tuned in to listen. And the song, just as they hoped it would be, was music to their ears.

**1988**   Adele Laurie Blue Adkins is born on May 5 in London, England.

**1991**   Attends her first music concert. Her mother takes her to see The Cure at Finsbury Park.

**1993**   Starts primary school in Tottenham.

**2002**   Is accepted into the BRIT School, a performing arts high school in London.

**2006**   Records a three-track demo for a school assignment that ends up changing her life. A friend posts the video on Myspace and managers from several record labels hear the music and approach Adele. When she finally responds, she is offered a recording contract.

**2008**   Releases her first album, titled *19*. The first single, "Hometown Glory," is an instant hit in England. When she performs "Chasing Pavements" and "Cold Shoulder" on *Saturday Night Live* later this year, more than 14 million people tune in to watch her.

**2009**   Wins Grammy Awards for Best New Artist and Best Female Pop Vocal Performance with her single "Hometown Glory." The BBC names her the Sound of 2008 for *19*.

**2011**   Releases her second album, *21*. It sells more than 352,000 copies in its first week. She becomes the second artist in history to have two top five singles and albums at the same time.

**2012**   Returns to the stage at the 54th Annual Grammy Awards. She also goes home with all six of the Grammys for which she was nominated. These include Album of the Year (*21*), Pop Solo Performance ("Someone Like You"), Pop Vocal Album (*21*), Record of the Year ("Rolling in the Deep"), Short Form Music Video ("Rolling in the Deep"), and Song of the Year ("Rolling in the Deep").

# DISCOGRAPHY

**2008** *19*

**2011** *21*

## SINGLES

2007 "Hometown Glory"

2008 "Chasing Pavements"
"Cold Shoulder"
"Make You Feel My
Love"

2010 "Rolling in the Deep"

2011 "Someone Like You"
"Rumour Has It"
"Set Fire to the Rain"

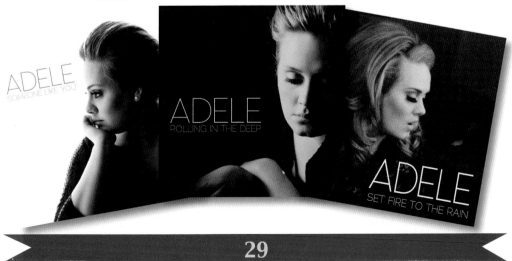

Newkey-Burden, Chas. *Adele: The Biography.* London, England: John Blake, 2012.

**Works Consulted**

Bamigboye, Baz. "Adele: Not Just Another Brit Pop Girl Next Door." *The Daily Mail,* January 24, 2008.

Barfield, Kahlana. "Violet Femme." *In Style,* April 2011.

Brockington, Ryan. "The Adele Interview That Brought Us to Tears." *New York Post,* February 17, 2011. http://www.nypost.com/p/blogs/popwrap/the_adele_interview_that_brought_jLcmX44rAmDLhlqbhIIXgO

Browne, David. "Inside Adele's Superstar Season." *Rolling Stone,* September 15, 2011.

Collis, Clark. "Adele, the New Queen of Heartbreak." *Entertainment Weekly,* April 15, 2011.

Herndon, Jessica. "Catching Up with . . . Adele." *People,* May 16, 2011.

Hill, Emily. "Adele's Father Admits: 'I Was a Rotten Dad . . .' " *The Daily Mail,* May 15, 2011.

Hughes, Sarah Anne. "Adele's Tour Rider Requests: Donations to Charity and No North American Beer." Celebritology, *Washington Post,* December 7, 2011.
http://www.washingtonpost.com/blogs/celebritology/post/adeles-tour-rider-requests-donations-to-charity-and-no-north-american-beer/2011/12/06/gIQAchSTcO_blog.html

"Interview: Adele, Singer." *The Scotland,* January 16, 2011.

Jones, Alan. "Adele's Chart Haul is Best Since Lennon." *Music Week,* February 26, 2011.

Knopper, Steve. "Adele Battles Vocal Issues." *Rolling Stone,* November 10, 2011.

Lewis, Pete. "Adele: Up Close and Personal." Blues & Soul Online.
http://www.bluesandsoul.com/feature/302/adele__up_close_and_personal/

McCormick, Neil. "Adele: 'I Want to Discover My Own Sound.' " *The Telegraph,* January 19, 2011.

Newkey-Burden. Chas. *Adele: The Biography*. London, England: John Blake, 2012.

Otey, Jim. "Adele." *Pollstar*, January 16, 2009.
http://www.pollstar.com/hotstar_article.aspx?ID=141927

Patterson, Sylvia. "Mad About The Girl." *The Observer*, January 26, 2008.

Sherwin, Adam. "The Secret to Adele's Success? No Festivals, Tweeting, or Selling Out." *The Independent*, May 24, 2011.
http://www.independent.co.uk/arts-entertainment/music/news/the-secret-of-adeles-success-no-festivals-tweeting-ndash-or-selling-out-2288168.html

Touré. "Best Soup Superstar: Adele." *Rolling Stone*, April 28, 2011.

Williams, Paul. "Adele to the Rescue." *Music Week*, April 16, 2011.

Wood, Mikael. "Adele: The Billboard Cover Story." *Billboard*, January 28, 2011.

**On the Internet**

Adele—Official Web Site
http://www.adele.tv/

Billboard.com—Adele
http://www.billboard.com/artist/adele/810846#/artist/adele/810846

Biography.com—Adele
http://www.biography.com/people/adele-20694679

INDEX